DEMCO

JE 031 BR

TIME

In this book, you will:

learn about telling time.

discover new words.

answer fun questions.

play a time-telling game.

find more time activities at the back of the book.

ENCYCLOPÆDIA
Britannica®

CHICAGO LONDON NEW DELHI PARIS SEOUL SYDNEY TAIPEI TOKYO

The sun rises.
Time to get dressed!

Breakfast time

Time to go.

Lunchtime

There is time for s

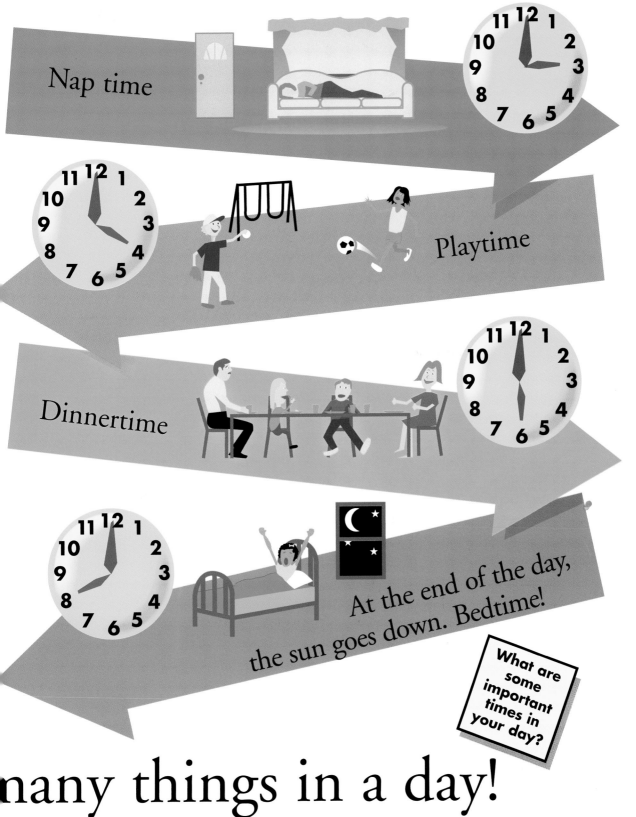

Nap time

Playtime

Dinnertime

At the end of the day, the sun goes down. Bedtime!

What are some important times in your day?

many things in a day!

When the sun is highest in the sky, we know it is noon.

We have many way

Early in the morning, bird. chirp and sing Roosters crow These sound tell us **dawn** has come

How did you know it was daytime when you woke up today?

4

f telling what time it is.

Long shadows across the ground tell us it is late afternoon.

What things do you see that tell you it is afternoon?

We know it is nighttime when the sun goes down and the stars come out.

How did you know it was time to go to bed last night?

Did you see the moon last night? What did it look like?

One night you can look up in the sky and see the moon, bright and full. As the nights go by, the moon seems to grow smaller. After many nights, you cannot see it at all. Then it grows full again. This is another way we know time is passing.

The time between two full moons is about four weeks.

Long ago, people had man

In some parts of the world, people rang bells in the morning. This told everyone it was time to go to work

ifferent ways of telling time.

some villages, people gathered together when they heard
e sound of beating drums. The drums meant it was time
r an important meeting.

This is a sundial.

The **sundial** was one of the first ways of telling time.

When the sun shines down on the sundial, the tall part of the sundial makes a shadow on the flat part.

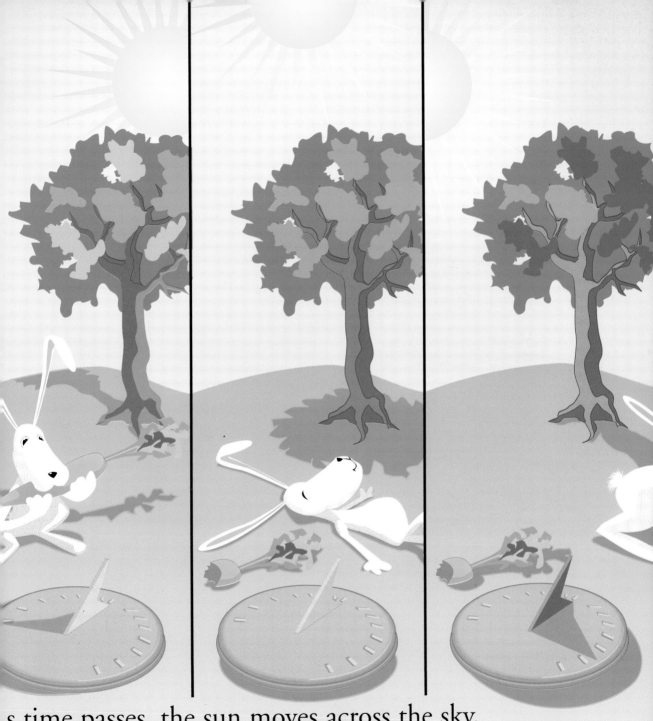

s time passes, the sun moves across the sky.
he shadow moves around the flat part of the sundial
s the sun moves in the sky. By looking at where the
hadow is, we know what time it is.

Today, many schools use bells to mark the time.
The bell rings when it is time for class to begin.
The bell rings again when class is over.

Traffic lights tell us when it is time for cars to stop and go. They tell us when it is time to walk safely across the street.

Most of the time, we us watches to tell us exactl

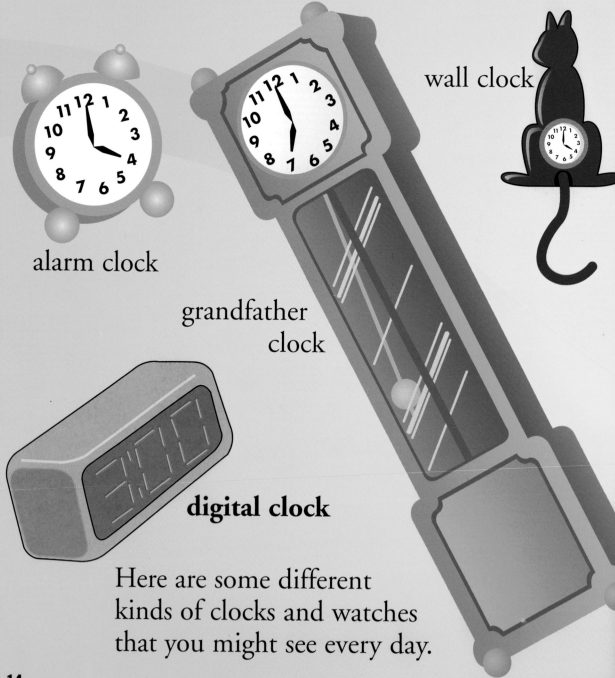

alarm clock

grandfather clock

wall clock

digital clock

Here are some different kinds of clocks and watches that you might see every day.

locks and
what time it is.

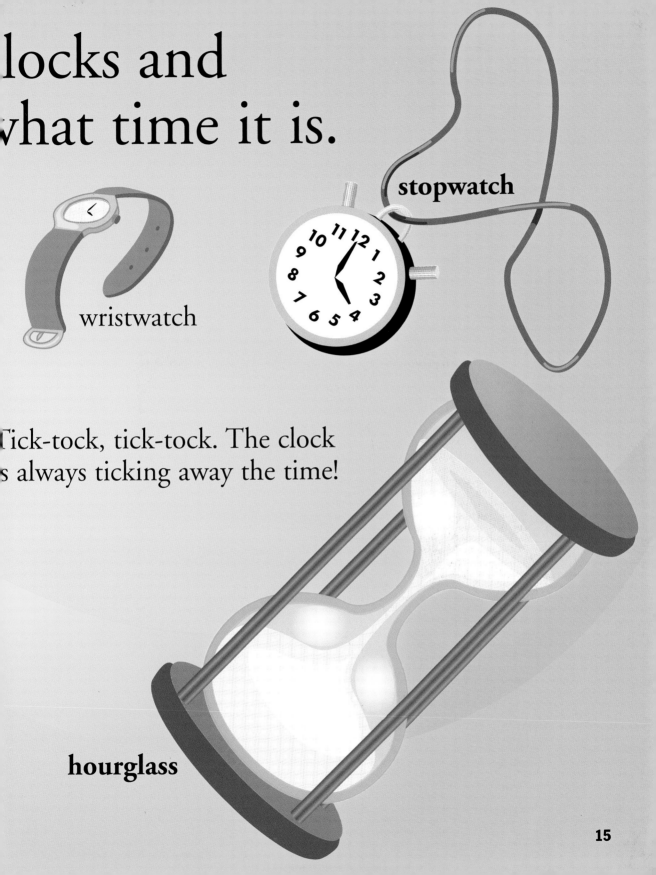

stopwatch

wristwatch

Tick-tock, tick-tock. The clock
s always ticking away the time!

hourglass

Here is a clock with a yellow face.

The clock has two hands and twelve numbers.
The little hand is red and the big hand is blue.

What time do you get up in the morning?

As time goes by, the hands on the clock move from number to number. On this clock, the big hand is pointing to 12. The little hand is pointing to 3. This means that the time is exactly 3 o'clock. The little hand always tells us what hour it is.

What time do you go to bed?

When the clock's little hand points to 2 and the big hand points to 12, it is exactly 2 o'clock.

When the little hand points to 11 and the big hand points to 12, it is exactly 11 o'clock.

When the little hand points to and the big hand points to 12, it exactly 5 o'cloc

Now look at the numbers that the big hand and the little hand are pointing to on the different clock faces here. What time is it on each clock?

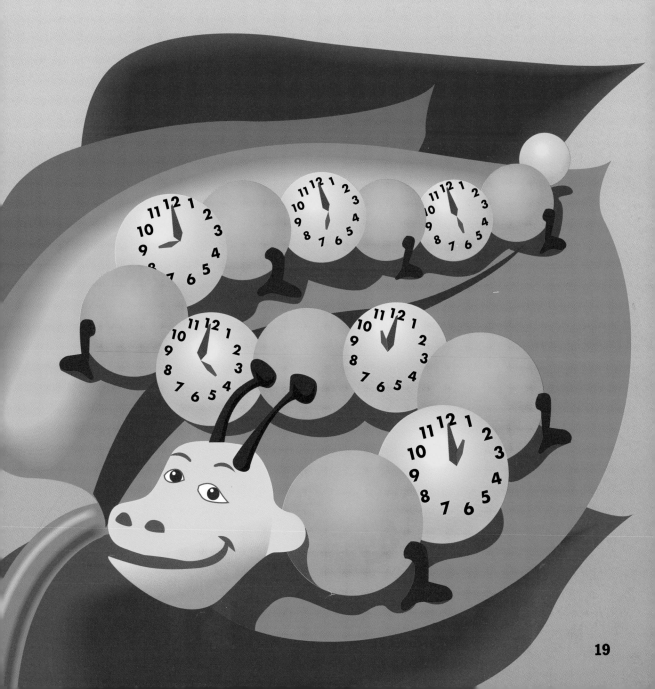

When the little hand starts at twelve and moves **twice**
past all the numbers on the clock face, we know that
a whole day and night have gone by. A new day begin

Every day of the week has a name.

 **Sunday**

Monday

 **Tuesday**

Wednesday

 **Thursday**

Friday

 **Saturday**

When all seven days have passed, a week has gone by.

What day of the week is it today?

There are about four weeks in ever

January

February

March

August

September

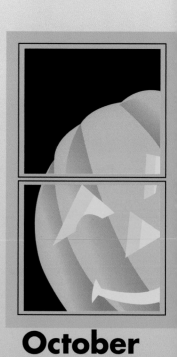

October

What is your favorite month? Why?

month. The months have names too.

April

May

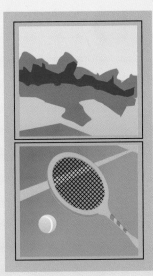

June

July

November

What month were you born?

December

When all twelve months have passed, a year has gone by. A year from now, you will be one year older.

Calendars are another way for us to tell how much tim
is passing. The calendar shows us every month of the
year. It shows us every day of each month too.

Calendars help us
remember holidays,
birthdays, and other
important dates.

Where have you seen calendars in your house?

We have so many different ways of knowing how much time has gone by!

How many ways of telling time can you find in this picture?

Here is a riddle.

You cannot see it or touch it, but without it, day would not turn into night.

It makes the seasons change. It makes you grow older.

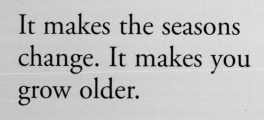

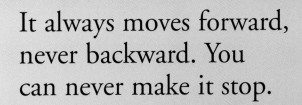

It always moves forward, never backward. You can never make it stop.

What is it?

TIME!

Minutes, hours, and days.
Days, weeks, and months.
Time is always passing!

TIME
GLOSSARY

dawn (dawn) the beginning of the day, when the sun rises and the world becomes light

digital clock (DIJ it uhl clok) a clock that shows the time in numbers instead of by hands or pointers that move around a clock face

hourglass (OUR glass) an instrument for measuring time that is made of glass, with two round compartments connected by a thin tube. Sand or water trickles from the top compartment to the bottom compartment in an hour's time.

stopwatch (stop wach) a watch that can be stopped or started in an instant, often used for timing races or other events

sundial (SUN dy uhl) an object that tells time by the position of a shadow made by the sun

twice (twys) two times

Fun Ways to Learn about T\ME

How Long Is a Minute?

1 You'll need a clock with a second hand or a stopwatch for this activity. Pick an activity that you would like to try to do for a whole minute—like hopping, drawing, singing. Then have a friend time you. Your friend should give you a "go!" signal to begin and say stop when exactly one minute has passed.

Were you able to do your activity for the whole minute? If not, how many seconds did you do it? Now, try again, doing a different activity, maybe swinging your arm back and forth. This time your friend will tell you when to start but won't tell you when the minute is up. Just stop doing your activity when you think one minute has passed. How close did you get?

Clock Count

2 How many ways of telling the time can you find in your own house? Count how many clocks you see in every room. (Don't forget digital clocks.) Do they all show the same time? What about other ways of telling time? Can you find an egg timer? A calendar? An alarm clock? An hourglass in a board game? A sundial? Which room in your house has the most ways of telling time?

Sundial Time

3 Make your own simple sundial! Take a thin, white (or any solid color) paper plate outside on a very sunny day and place it on the ground. Use a full-size pencil to mark a dot at the very center of the plate. Then push the pencil down through the dot and into the ground to keep the plate in place. Now start watching a regular clock. At the beginning of every hour, go outside and mark the plate exactly where you see the end of the pencil's shadow. If you begin at 10 o'clock in the morning, write the number 10 on the shadow line. Do this each time a new hour begins for as many hours as you can. The next day you won't have to go inside to know what time it is—just look at your sundial!

Helping Children Get the Most out of the *TIME* Volume

Children begin to understand the concept of time, even before they can tell time, by understanding the relationship between events and time — for instance, you can point out the things that happen at the same time every day, or how long it takes to do something, such as bake cookies or drive to the park. Recognizing that things can come one after another prepares a child for later important tasks too, such as telling time, doing math, and reading. Throughout a day there are many opportunities to help children learn about the concept of time. The activities on the previous page are meant to further that understanding.

How Long Is a Minute? If you don't have a stopwatch, you'll need a clock with a second hand for this activity. Let the children pick what they want to do or suggest something, like hopping, drawing, humming, singing. Before beginning, let them watch the second hand sweep around once so that they can get a sense of how long a minute is. Another fun and easy way for children to guess when a minute is up is to have them simply raise their hand or close their eyes until they think a minute has gone by. No matter when they stop, tell them exactly how much time has passed.

Clock Count. Make a game out of hunting for timepieces around the house. You can accompany your younger children and give hints or point out timepieces they overlook. As an additional activity, you might ask an older child to make a list of how many timepieces are in each room, then add up the total. Before or after this activity, you can show them an analog and a digital clock and explain how they work. Looking at the two clocks side by side will help them grasp the difference.

Sundial Time. Learning about sundials is a lot of fun for older children. If necessary, remind them when each new hour begins so they can go outside and add a mark to their sundial. Later, point out that as the pencil's shadow moves to each mark on the dial, a new hour begins. You can expand this activity by measuring the child's shadow each hour. Explain how as the sun gets higher in the sky shadows get shorter, and as the sun gets lower in the sky shadows become longer. This is another way that the passage of time is marked.

Illustrations by Jerry A. Kraus.

© 2005 by Encyclopædia Britannica, Inc.

International Standard Book Number: 1-59339-102-1

Britannica Discovery Library:
Volume 11: Time 2005

Britannica.com may be accessed on the Internet at http://www.britannica.com.